D0292613

NEVER GET TOO PERSONALLY INVOLVED WITH YOUR OWN LIFE

Sheed Andrews and McMeel, Inc.
Subsidiary of Universal Press Syndicate
Kansas City

"Ziggy" is syndicated internationally by
UNIVERSAL PRESS SYNDICATE

Copyright © 1975 by

UNIVERSAL PRESS SYNDICATE

All rights reserved. Printed in the United States of America. No part of this book may be used or reproduced in any manner whatsoever without permission except in the case of reprints in the context of reviews. For information write Sheed Andrews and McMeel, Inc., 6700 Squibb Road, Mission, Kansas 66202.

ISBN: 0-8362-0623-1
Library of Congress Catalog Card Number 75-16558

for YOU
my "ZIGGY" friend

WELL FRIEND...
WHAT'S IT GONNA BE TODAY..?
..ARE YOU WITH ME ? OR AGAINST ME ??

LITTER

LOST & FOUND
...SAYS HE'S LOST HIS SENSE OF DIRECTION IN LIFE ...WANTS TO KNOW IF WE CAN HELP HIM

ENDANGERED SPECiES

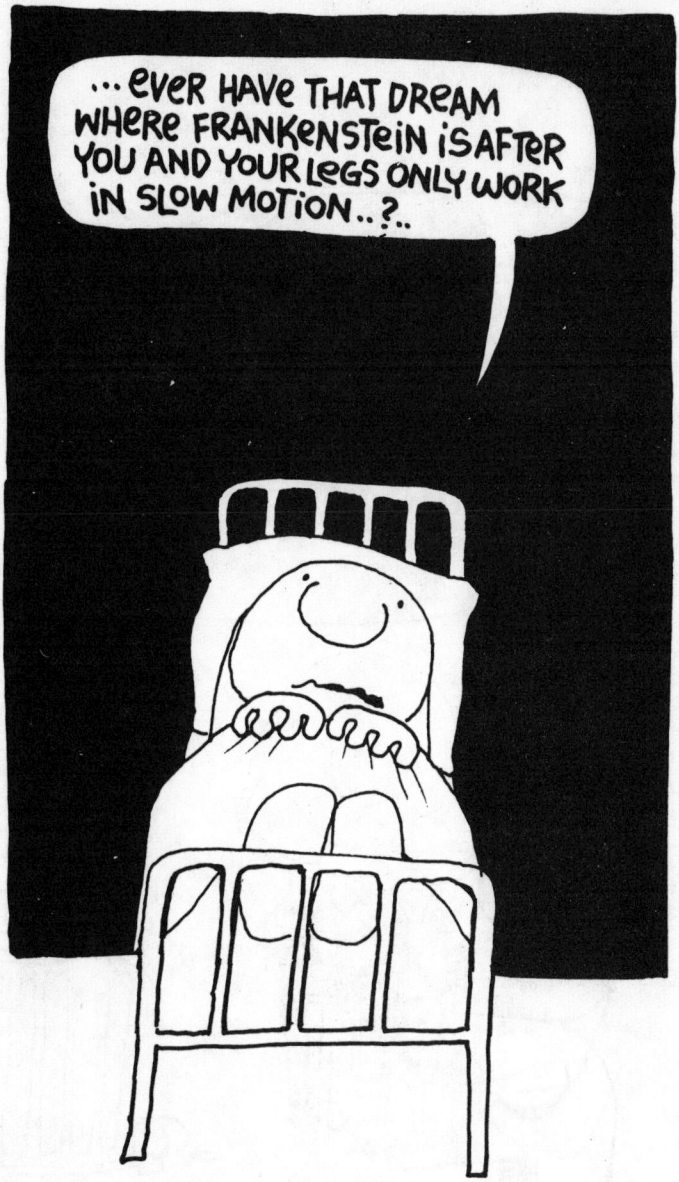
...EVER HAVE THAT DREAM WHERE FRANKENSTEIN IS AFTER YOU AND YOUR LEGS ONLY WORK IN SLOW MOTION..?..

TAKING OUT THE GARBAGE IS VERY THERAPEUTIC
...IT HELPS KEEP ONE IN TOUCH WITH REALITY !!

YOUR HOROSCOPE
YOUR CHANCES FOR HAVING A GOOD DAY CAN BE IMPROVED CONSIDERABLY IF YOU JUST FORGET IT . . . GO BACK TO BED . . . AND STAY THERE!!

IF I EVER HAD ANY "GET UP AND GO"
...IT GOT UP AND WENT

ONE GOOD THING ABOUT BEING A NOBODY IS THAT YOU NEVER HAVE TO WORRY ABOUT HAVING AN IDENTITY CRISIS...

i LOVE FOOTBALL... except WHEN THEY GET IN A HUDDLE...
... i ALWAYS THINK THEY'RE TALKING ABOUT ME !!
YEA
13

I THINK I'M SUFFERING FROM A CHARISMA DEFICIENCY!

CANINE
OBEDIENCE
SCHOOL

...THERE BUT FOR THE GRACE OF GOD GO i.....
...THERE BUT FOR THE GRACE OF GOD GO i.....

...LOOKS LIKE A...
"PUT ON MY FRANK SINATRA RECORDS AND FEEL SORRY FOR MYSELF"
KIND OF DAY....

ABOUT THE ONLY THING THAT HAPPENS TO ME ON WEEK-ENDS IS...

...I GET TWO DAYS OLDER!!

LIFE'S A LITTLE LESS COMPLICATED WHEN YOU LIVE ALONE.....

FOR ONE THING THERE'S NEVER ANY QUESTION ABOUT WHO DIDN'T JIGGLE THE HANDLE ON THE "JOHN"!!

LIVE LIFE ONE LUMP AT A TIME

WISHING WELL
SPLOOSH

WISHING WELL
i WISH i KNeW HOW To SWIM...

...IT'S BEEN ONE OF THOSE DAYS !!

FIRST I GET INTO A BIG FIGHT WITH MY WIFE... THEN I GO OUT TO START THE CAR AND FIND I HAVE A FLAT TIRE...

...NEXT I GET A PARKING TICKET RIGHT OUTSIDE MY OWN BARBER SHOP...

iF YOU BREAK iT
..YOU BOUGHT iT !

... AND THERE IS SOME PROBABILITY OF TODAY, AND AN 80% CHANCE OF TOMORROW..

WELL...
..IT'S YOU AND ME AGAINST THE WORLD,
...PERSONALLY I THINK WE'RE GOING TO GET CREAMED !!

PLEASE USE
REVOLVING
DOOR

i DON'T LIVE IT UP MUCH
...BUT i DON'T HAVE MUCH TO LIVE DOWN EITHER !!

BEWARE
OF

iM HeRe To FiX THe AiR CONDiTiONeR!

PUBLIC
SQUARE

...YOU KNOW TIMES ARE BAD, WHEN YOU CALL DIAL-A-PRAYER, AND FIND THAT THEY HAVE AN UNLISTED NUMBER...

..I GO THROUGH LIFE WITH THE FEELING THAT I'M THE ONE WEARING THE "KICK ME" SIGN...

..YOU KNOW YOU'RE "OUT OF IT"
WHEN YOU CAN'T RECOGNIZE
ANY OF THE SONGS
OR SINGERS ON
THE JUKE BOX!!

ES REST ROOM

OUR FUTURE IS SHAPED BY OUR PAST....
...SO BE VERY CAREFUL WHAT YOU DO IN YOUR PAST !!

I WONDER HOW UPCREEK AIRLINES IS GOING TO APOLOGIZE FOR THIS LITTLE INCONVENIENCE ?..

..LOOKS LIKE THE SEAS
AREN'T GOING TO BE ANY
TOO FRIENDLY EITHER !!

WHAT DID i EVER DO TO DESERVE THIS ??!!
WANNA LIST??

GETTING IT ALL TOGETHER

i GeT SO CONFUSeD
SOMeTIMeS, i DON'T
KNOW WHiCH eND iS UP

....WHiCH ReALLY MAKeS
iT DiFFiCULT WHeN i TRY
TO SiT DOWN

WE'LL HAVE TO KEEP HIM FOR A COUPLE OF DAYS...
...DOES HE PREFER A PRIVATE OR A SEMI-PRIVATE ROOM ??

MONDAY WAS MISERABLE..
TUESDAY WAS TERRIBLE...
WEDNESDAY WAS WORSE..
..THURSDAY WAS HORRIBLE
...NOW WHAT ??
T.G.I.F.

I REALLY HATE TO LEAVE...
...BUT I ONLY HAVE 10 MINUTES LEFT ON MY 8 HOUR DEODORANT!

SOMETIMES I FEEL LIKE I'M ON THE EXPRESS ELEVATOR OF LIFE
...GOING DOWN.

I THINK I COULD ENJOY THE DAY MORE ... IF IT DIDN'T START SO EARLY !!

STAY ON "THE STRAIGHT AND NARROW" ZIG...
...THAT WAY YOU'LL NEVER HAVE TO WORRY ABOUT BUMPING INTO ANYONE !!

I'M STRAPPED ... CAN YOU LET ME HAVE FIVE UNTIL DOOMSDAY?
PREPARE TO MEET THY DOOM!
THE END IS NEAR

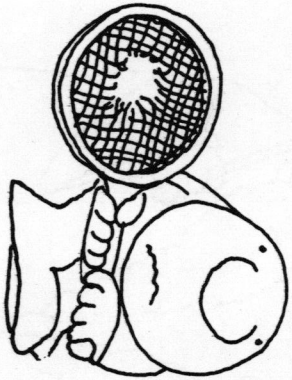

...SNOW JUST DOESNT TASTE LIKE IT USED TO!

...I WONDER IF THERE'S A GREAT BIG "LOST AND FOUND" IN THE SKY?

...WHERE EVERYTHING WE EVER LOST IS WAITING FOR US TO COME AND FIND IT....

..DO YOU WANT YOUR HAMBURGER BURNT OR WELL BURNT ?

FIRST THING I DO WHEN I WAKE UP IN THE MORNING IS READ THE OBITUARIES ... IF MY NAME ISN'T THERE, I GET DRESSED, AND START ANOTHER DAY!!

LiFe
SWiNGS

NATURE IS ALMOST PERFECT...
EXCEPT FOR ONE THING....
...IF IT WERE UP TO ME,
I DON'T THINK I WOULD HAVE
PUT IT ALL OUTSIDE !!

i never met
a nobody that
i didn't like...

i've never been able to catch them at it...
...but i swear they reproduce in there when i'm not lookin !!

ONE WAY

IN THE GREAT SANDWICH OF LIFE
THERE'S SURE A LOT OF BOLOGNA!!

OH WELL.. WE CAN'T ALL BE WINNERS

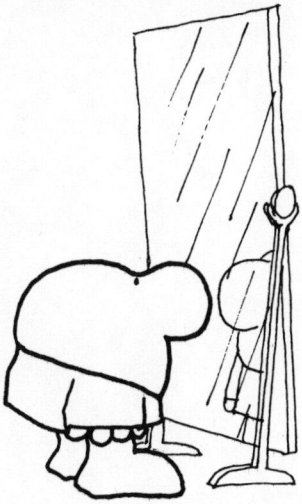

ALSO RAN
LAST PLACE
NICE GUY AWARD FOR FINISHING LAST
LOSERS CUP
CONSOLATION PRIZE

YOUR HIGHWAY
TAX DOLLARS
AT WORK

THE ONLY PLACE
I DON'T FEEL LIKE
A LOSER..
..IS ON THE
BATHROOM SCALES!!

I ALWAYS SEEM TO HAVE TROUBLE GETTING SERVED IN RESTAURANTS..
...MAYBE IT'S BECAUSE I ALWAYS LOOK LIKE I'VE ALREADY EATEN!
Tom Wilson

WHEN YOU REACH MIDDLE AGE...
...ALL YOU EXERCISE IS CAUTION !!

..eR..UH...
BeeN WAiTiNG LONG?
BUS
STOP

IN THE
YELLOW PAGES
OF LIFE
...IM LISTED UNDER
MISCELLANEOUS !!

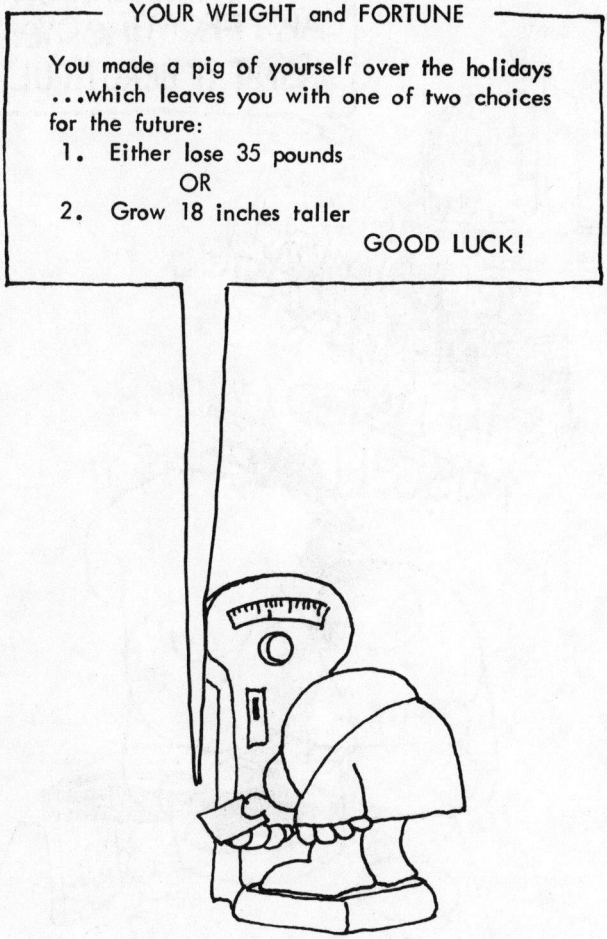
YOUR WEIGHT and FORTUNE
You made a pig of yourself over the holidays ...which leaves you with one of two choices for the future:
1. Either lose 35 pounds
OR
2. Grow 18 inches taller
GOOD LUCK!

NOW..REMOVE YOUR CAKE FROM THE OVEN ...ISN'T IT BEAUTIFUL ?!
wilcox
CAKE O MAKE

...everytime i sit back and ponder the highlights of my life...
i doze off...

GOODNIGHT
MOTHER NATURE

..ONE OF THE REALLY GREAT DISAPPOINTMENTS IN LIFE,
..IS GETTING AN INVITATION TO LUNCH FROM AN OLD FRIEND YOU HAVEN'T SEEN IN YEARS,
... AND FIND OUT HE'S SELLING INSURANCE!!!
©1975 Universal Press Syndicate

GATE A
BOX SEATS
BOX
21
21

YOU DON'T HAVE TO BE ALONE TO BE LONELY...
...BUT THAT'S WHEN YOU FEEL IT THE MOST!!
Tom Wilson

...THERE MUST BE A BETTER WAY TO SPEND MY EVENINGS THAN TO JUST SIT AROUND HOPING FOR A WRONG NUMBER...